Recipes for Homemade Bread and Cakes

Bakery at Home

Lea F. Lehman

BREAD

Home-made bread is very much more palatable and more nutritious than baker's bread and it is worth while to spend time and effort in its preparation.

To make good bread, it is necessary to have good flour, fresh yeast and the liquid used in moistening must be neither too hot nor too cold or the bread will not rise properly.

FLOUR

The housekeeper should know about the different kinds of flour. We get the bread flour from the spring wheat; the pastry flour from the winter wheat.

Bread flour contains more gluten than pastry flour and is used for bread on that account. Pastry flour having less gluten and slightly more starch is more suitable for pastry and cake mixtures and is used wherever softness and lightness are desired.

Graham flour is the whole kernel of wheat ground.

Entire wheat flour is the flour resulting from the grinding of all but the outer layer of the wheat.

Rye flour is next best to wheat flour for bread making, but is generally combined with wheat flour, since by itself it makes a sticky bread.

Cornmeal is also combined with wheat flour.

Variety bread is composed of bread flour, rye flour and cornmeal combined in one loaf.

If flour is musty; it is not kosher and must be destroyed. Keep flour either in tins or barrels in a dry atmosphere.

YEAST

In cities where fresh compressed yeast can be obtained, it is not worth while to prepare one's own.

Compressed yeast is always in proper condition to use until it becomes soft, often the yeast cakes are slightly discolored, but this does not affect the yeast, being caused by the oxidation of the starch in the cake.

Keep yeast in cool place.

HOME MADE YEAST

Grate six large raw potatoes, have ready a gallon of water in which you have boiled one and one-half cups of hops. Strain through a fine hair sieve, boiling hot, over the potatoes, stirring well, or the mixture will thicken like starch. Add a scant cup of sugar and one-half cup of salt. When cold, add a yeast cake or a cup of fresh yeast. Let it stand until a thick foam rises on the top. Bottle in a few days. If kept in a cool place, this yeast will last a long time. Use one cup of yeast for one large baking. In making yeast, from time to time, use a cup of the same with which to start the new yeast.

One cup of liquid yeast is equal to one cake of compressed yeast.

When yeast is not obtainable to start the fermentation in making yeast, mix a thin batter of flour and water, and let it stand in a warm place until it is full of bubbles. This ferment has only half the strength of yeast so double the amount must be used.

TO MAKE BREAD

Try the yeast always by setting to raise in a cup of lukewarm water or milk, if you use compressed yeast add salt and sugar.

If it rises in the course of ten or fifteen minutes, the yeast is fit to use. In making bread always use sifted flour. Set a sponge with lukewarm milk or water, keeping it covered in a warm place until very light, then mold this sponge by adding flour, until very light into one large ball, then knead well and steadily for twenty minutes. Set to rise again in a warm place free from drafts, and when it has risen to double its former bulk, take a knife, cut through the dough in several places, then place this dough on a baking board which has been sprinkled with flour. Work with the palm of the hand, always kneading towards the centre of the ball (the dough must rebound like a rubber ball). When this leaves the board and the hands perfectly clean the dough may be formed into loaves or rolls.

Place in pan, greased slightly with a good oil, let rise until the imprint of the finger does not remain, and bake.

The oven for baking bread should be hot enough to brown a teaspoon of flour in five minutes.

If baked in a coal range, the fire must be just the proper heat so as not to have to add fuel or shake the stove.

If baked in a gas range, light oven to full heat five minutes before putting the bread in the oven, and bake in a moderately hot oven forty-five minutes, unless the loaves are very large when one hour will be the proper time.

When taken from the oven, the bread may be wrapped in a clean towel wrung out of warm water (this prevents the crust from becoming hard); place bread in slanting position or allow it to cool on a wire rack.

WHITE BREAD

Set the dough at night and bake early in the morning; take one-half cake of compressed yeast, set in a cup of lukewarm milk or water adding a teaspoon of salt and a tablespoon of sugar. Let this rise, if it does not, the yeast is not fresh or good. Measure eight cups of sifted flour into a deep bread bowl, add one teaspoon of salt; make a depression in the centre, pour in the risen yeast and one cup of lukewarm milk or water. In winter be sure that the bowl, flour, milk, in fact everything has been thoroughly warmed before mixing. Mix the dough slowly with a wooden spoon and then knead as directed.

This amount will make two loaves, either twisted or in small bread pans. Bake forty-five minutes in a moderate oven.

If the bread is set in the morning use a cake of compressed yeast and bake the loaves in the afternoon.

INDIVIDUAL LOAVES

Make dough according to the above recipe. Work small pieces of dough into strands a finger long, and take three strands for each loaf. Make small as possible, brush with beaten egg; or sweetened water and sprinkle with poppy seed (mohn). Allow them to rise before setting them in the oven. These are called "Vienna loaves" and are used at weddings, parties and for the Succoth festival in the Succah.

If one-half cake of yeast has been used, the half cake of yeast which is left over, can be kept in good condition several days by rewrapping it in the tinfoil and keeping it in a cool, dry place.

COFFEE CAKES (KUCHEN)

RENDERED BUTTER

Procure as much country or Western butter as desired, you may get several pounds of it when it is cheap during the summer; or any butter unfit for table use may be made sweet and good for cooking purposes and will last for months, if prepared in the following manner: Place the butter in a deep, iron kettle, filling only half full to prevent boiling over. Set it on the fire where it will simmer slowly for several hours. Watch carefully that it does not boil over. Do not stir it, but from time to time skim it. When perfectly clear, and all the salt and sediment has settled at the bottom, the butter is done. Set aside a few minutes, then strain into stone jars through a fine sieve, and when cold tie up tightly with paper and cloth. Keep in a cool, dry place.

COFFEE CAKE (KUCHEN) DOUGH

Soak one-half ounce of yeast in one-half cup of lukewarm milk; when dissolved put in a bowl, or round agate pan, and stir in one cup of sifted flour, one teaspoon of sugar and one-fourth teaspoon of salt, mix thoroughly, and put in a warm place (not hot) to rise, from one to two hours.

When well risen, cream well together one cup of sugar and three-fourths cup of butter, then add three eggs, five cups of sifted flour, one cup of milk and one teaspoon of salt, mix together until light, then stir in the risen yeast, and with a spoon work well for ten minutes, and set aside to rise again, five or six hours or all night. Dough should not be very stiff. When well risen it can be used for cinnamon cake, pies or pocket books. This recipe makes one large cinnamon cake, three pies, and about one dozen pocket books. If set at night use half the quantity of yeast.

KAFFEE KUCHEN (CINNAMON)

Butter long and broad cake-pans thoroughly, roll out enough dough to cover them, and let it rise about half an hour before baking, then brush it well with melted butter. Sprinkle sugar and cinnamon on top and some chopped almonds. Take a small lump of butter, a very little flour, some sugar and cinnamon and rub it between the hands until it is like lumps of almonds, then strew on top of cakes.

CINNAMON ROLLS OR SCHNECKEN

Take half the kitchen dough. Roll one-half inch thick and spread well with melted butter. Sprinkle generously with scraped maple, brown or granulated sugar and cinnamon, then roll. Cut the roll into equal parts about one inch thick, place close together endwise in a spider, generously buttered, spread with one-fourth inch layer of brown, or maple sugar. Let rise until light, and bake ten to twenty minutes in a hot oven, a golden brown. Invert the spider, remove rolls and serve caramel side up.

ABGERUEHRTER KUGELHOPF

Soak one-half ounce of yeast or one cake compressed yeast in a very little lukewarm milk; add a pinch of salt and one tablespoon of sugar, stir it up smooth and set back of the stove to rise. In the meantime rub a scant cup of butter and a scant cup of powdered sugar to a cream, add gradually the yolks of four eggs, one at a time and add also the grated peel of a lemon. Sift two cups of flour into a bowl, make a depression in the centre, pour in, the yeast, one cup of lukewarm milk, and make a light batter of this. Add the creamed butter and eggs and stir until it forms blisters and leaves the bowl clean. Take one-half cup of cleaned and seeded dark raisins and cut up some citron very fine. Dredge flour over them before adding, and if necessary, add more flour to the dough, which should be of the consistency of cup cake batter. Last add the stiffly-beaten whites of the eggs. Place in a well-greased long or round pan with tube in centre; let rise until double in bulk, and bake in moderate oven until browned and thoroughly done.

PLAIN BUNT OR NAPF KUCHEN

Take one cake compressed yeast, add a pinch of salt, one tablespoon of sugar, and about two tablespoons of lukewarm water. Stir the yeast until it is a smooth paste and set it in a warm place to rise. Sift two and one-half cups of flour (use the same size cup for measuring everything you are going to use in your cake), make a depression in the centre, stir in the yeast and a scant cup of lukewarm milk, make batter, and let it rise until you have prepared the following: Rub one-half cup of butter and three-fourths cup of powdered sugar to a cream, just as for cup cake, then add gradually one egg at a time, using three altogether, and stirring all the time in one direction. Work in the risen batter two or three spoons at a time between each egg. Grate in the peel of a lemon or an orange. Butter the bunt-form well (do this always before you begin to work). Blanched almonds may be set in the grooves of the cake-form after buttering it. Put in the dough, set it in a warm place and let it rise for an hour and a half or two hours. Bake in a moderate oven one full hour, covered at first.

CHOCOLATE COFFEE CAKE

Pour a bunt kitchen dough into long, well-buttered tins, and when baked remove from the oven and cover thickly with boiled chocolate icing.

POCKET BOOKS

Take as much of the coffee cake dough as you desire, lay it on a well-floured biscuit board and mix just enough more flour with it to enable you to roll it out without sticking to the board. Roll out about one-fourth inch thick and cut the dough in squares about as long as your finger.

Beat the yolk of one egg and two tablespoons of milk together; wet each square well with the mixture, lay one raisin in the centre (after the seed has been removed from it), sprinkle thickly with sugar and cinnamon mixed together, then put a small dab of butter on top. Catch the four corners of each square together, so that the inside is protected. Lay the pocket books, not too closely together, in a greased pan and set aside to rise. When well risen bake in a moderately hot oven until well baked and browned nicely.

BOLA

Make a good, rich bread dough. Let it rise overnight; next morning; mix with dough two eggs; one-half pound of butter well kneaded; stand by fire until well risen. When risen, roll out into thin sheets and sprinkle with chopped almonds, citron, cinnamon and plenty of brown sugar and lumps of butter all through; roll up like jelly-roll, cut in pieces a finger long, grease pan, stand pieces in centre, others around and let rise before baking. Watch it well while baking.

FRENCH COFFEE CAKE (SAVARIN)

Soak one cake of compressed yeast in a little lukewarm water or milk. Put the yeast in a cup, add two tablespoons of lukewarm water, a pinch of salt and one tablespoon of sugar, stir it up well with a spoon and set back of the stove to rise. Rub one-half cup of butter to a cream, add one-third cup of powdered sugar and stir constantly in one direction. Add the yolks of four eggs, one at a time, and the grated peel of a lemon. Sift two cups of flour into a bowl, make a depression in the centre of the flour, pour in the yeast and one cup of lukewarm milk. Stir and make a light batter of this. Add the creamed butter and eggs, stir until it forms blisters and leaves the bowl clean; one-half cup of dark raisins, one-half cup of pounded almonds and a little citron, cut up very fine, and last the stiff-beaten whites of the eggs. Fill your cake forms which have been well-greased, set in a warm place to rise until double in bulk, about forty-five minutes, and bake in a moderate oven forty-five minutes. Fill the centre with whipped cream and serve with rum sauce.

BABA À LA PARISIENNE

Prepare the yeast as above; cream a scant cup of butter with four tablespoons of sugar, the grated peel of a lemon, add five eggs, one at a time, stirring each egg a few minutes before you add the next. Have ready two cups of sifted flour and add two spoonfuls between each egg until all is used. Make a soft dough of the yeast, a scant cup of lukewarm milk, add two spoonfuls between each egg until all is used up, a pinch of salt, and one cup of flour. Let it rise for fifteen minutes. Now mix all well, rub the form with butter, and blanch one-half cup of almonds, cut into long strips and strew all over the form. Fill in the mixture or cake batter, let it rise two hours and bake very slowly.

MOHN (POPPY SEED) ROLEY POLEY

Roll out a piece of dough large enough to cover your whole baking-board, roll thin. Let it rise until you have prepared the filling; grind one cup of black poppy seed in a coffee-mill as tight as possible and clean it well, throw away the first bit you grind so as not to have the coffee taste; put it on to boil with one cup of milk, add two tablespoons of butter, one-half cup of seeded raisins, one-half cup of walnuts or almonds chopped up fine, two tablespoons of molasses or syrup, and a little citron cut up fine. When thick, set it away to cool, and if not sweet enough add more sugar and flavor with vanilla. When this mixture has cooled, spread on the dough which has risen by this time. Take up one corner and roll it up, into a long roll, like a jelly-roll, put in a greased pan and let it rise an hour, then spread butter on top and bake very slowly. Let it get quite brown, so as to bake through thoroughly. When cold cut up in slices, as many as you are going to use at one time only.

MOHN WACHTEL

Take coffee cake dough. Let the dough rise again; for an hour, spread with a poppy seed mixture, after cutting into squares, fold into triangles and pinch the edges together. Lay in well-buttered pans, about two inches apart, and let them rise again, spread with poppy seed filling. Take one-half pound of poppy seed (mohn) which have previously been soaked in milk and then ground, add one-quarter of a pound of sugar and the yolks of three eggs. Stir this all together in one direction until quite thick and then stir in the beaten whites to which you must add two ounces of sifted flour and one-quarter of a pound of melted butter. Fill the tartlets and bake. The poppy seed filling in Mohn Roley Poley may be used in the Mohn Wachtel if so desired.

MOHNTORTS

Line a deep pie-plate with a thin sheet of kuchen dough, let it rise about half an hour, then fill with a poppy seed filling same as used with Mohn Wachtel. Fill the pie-plates and bake.

SMALL MOHN CAKES

Roll coffee cake dough out quite thin, spread with melted butter (a brush is best for this purpose). Let it rise a little while, then sprinkle well with one cup of sugar, add one-half pound of ground poppy seed moistened with one-half cup of water, cut into strips about an inch wide and four-inches long; roll and put in a well-buttered pan to rise, leaving enough space between each and brush, with butter. Bake in moderate oven at first, then increase the heat; bake slowly.

BERLINER PFANNKUCHEN (PURIM KRAPFEN)

Take one and one-half cups of flour, a pinch of salt sifted into a deep bowl, one cup of lukewarm milk and three-fourths cake of compressed yeast which has been, dissolved in a little warm water and sugar. Stir into a dough, cover with a towel and set away in a warm place to rise. When well risen, take one-half cup of butter, one cup of sugar, a little salt and rub to a cream. Add two eggs well beaten, stir all well and add the risen dough, one teaspoon of salt and work in gradually five cups of sifted flour and the grated peel of a lemon. Stir the dough till it blisters and leaves the dish perfectly clean at the sides. Let the dough rise slowly for about two hours (all yeast dough is better if it rises slowly). Take a large baking-board, flour well and roll out the dough on it as thin as a double thickness of pasteboard. When it is all rolled out, cut with a round cutter the size of a tumbler. When all the dough has been cut out, beat up an egg. Spread the beaten egg; on the edge of each cake (spread only a few at a time for they would get too dry if all were done at once). Then put one-half teaspoon of marmalade, jam or jelly on the cake. Put another cake on top of one already spread, having cut it with a cutter a little bit smaller than the one used in the first place. This makes them stick better and prevents the preserves coming out while cooking. Set all away on a floured board or pan about two inches apart. Spread the top of each cake with melted butter and let them rise from one to two hours. When ready to fry, heat at least two pounds of rendered butter or any good vegetable oil in a deep iron kettle. Try the butter with a small piece of dough. If it rises immediately, put in the doughnuts. In putting them in, place the side that is up on the board down in the hot butter. Do not crowd them in the kettle as they require room to rise and spread. Cover them with a lid. In a few seconds uncover. If they are light brown, turn them over on the other side but do not cover them again. When done they will have a white stripe around the centre. Take them up with a perforated skimmer, lay on a large platter, sprinkle with pulverized sugar. If the butter gets too hot take from the fire a minute. These are best eaten fresh.

The doughnuts may be baked in moderately hot oven and when half done glazed with sugar and white of egg.

TOPFA DALKELN. CHEESE CAKES (HUNGARIAN)

Take one-half ounce of yeast, mix with a little scalded milk which has cooled to lukewarm, one-half cup of flour and put aside in a warm place to rise. Allow two cups of scalded milk to become lukewarm. Add one pound of flour (four cups sifted flour) to the risen sponge, then the two cups of milk, mix these very well, cover with a cloth and put aside in a warm place to rise. Take one pound of sweet pot cheese, a pinch of salt, three egg yolks, rind of one lemon, one-half cup of light colored raisins and sugar to taste; mix very well and add the beaten whites and mix thoroughly. When the dough is very well risen, place on a pastry board, roll out and spread with melted butter, fold these edges over to the middle, then the top and bottom over, roll again and spread with butter, fold all sides in once more, roll, spread with butter, repeat the folding, roll out to one-half inch thickness, cut in three-inch squares, place a tablespoon of the cheese mixture in the centre of each square, fold over opposite corners, spread egg white over the top of each pocket, let rise fifteen minutes or one-half hour and bake in a hot oven; when they are well risen, lower heat and bake to a golden brown. This will make about thirty cakes. The dough in the above may be used with the following filling:

Boil and stone one-half pound of prunes, mash to a pulp, sweeten, add the grated peel of a lemon, some cinnamon, etc., and put one teaspoon of this into each square. Take up the corners, fasten them firmly, also pinch all along the edges and lay in a buttered pan, let them rise half an hour before baking. Spread them with melted butter, and bake a nice brown.

PUFFS (PURIM)

Make the dough same as for Berliner Pfannkuchen, and when well risen roll out on a floured board one-half inch thick, cut in triangles, lay on floured dishes or board to rise. When well risen, drop into a deep kettle of boiling butter and with a spoon baste with the butter until brown; remove with a perforated skimmer and sprinkle with powdered sugar.

KINDLECH

Into a large bowl sift one pound of fine flour. Make a depression in the centre and pour into it one yeast cake dissolved in a little milk. Let this remain until the milk and yeast have risen a little. Stir in the surrounding flour together with three well-beaten eggs, a quarter of a pound of butter, six ounces of sugar, a pinch of salt and two cups of lukewarm milk. Knead the whole into a smooth dough.

Roll this out very lightly on a well-floured board, brush over with a feather dipped in melted butter and strew thickly with chopped almonds, sultanas and currants. Next fold over about three fingers' width of the dough. Brush the upper surface of this fold with melted butter and strew with mixed fruit and almonds. Fold over again and repeat the operation until the whole of the dough is folded up in layer somewhat resembling a flattened, roley poley pudding. Brush the top well with another feather dipped in beaten egg and cut the whole into thick slices or fingers. Let them stand for half an hour and then bake for an hour in a rather slow oven.

A CHEAP COFFEE CAKE

This German coffee cake is made by kneading into a pint of bread dough one well-beaten egg, one-half cup of sugar, and a generous tablespoon of butter. The mixture is rolled flat, placed in a shallow pan, let rise again until very light, sprinkled with finely chopped nuts, dusted over with sugar and cinnamon and baked in a quick oven.

BOHEMIAN KOLATCHEN

Make kuchen dough. Add a little cinnamon and mace and one teaspoon of anise seed, well pounded, or flavor to taste. Let rise till very light, then take out on mixing board and roll out to about one-half inch in thickness. Cut in rounds three inches in diameter and lay on a well-buttered pan, pressing down the centre of each so as to raise a ridge around the edge. When well risen, brush the top over with stiffly-beaten white of an egg and sprinkle with granulated sugar.

ZWIEBACK

Scald one-half cup of milk and when lukewarm add to one cake of compressed yeast. Add one-fourth cup of sugar, one-fourth cup of melted butter, one-half teaspoon of salt and three eggs unbeaten, one-half teaspoon of powdered anise and enough flour to handle. Let rise until light. Make into oblong rolls the length of middle finger and place together in a buttered pan in parallel rows, two inches apart. Let rise again and bake twenty minutes. When cold, cut in one-half inch slices and brown evenly in the oven.

SOUR CREAM KOLATCHEN

Cream one-half cup of butter, add five yolks, two tablespoons of sugar, grated rind of a lemon, one cup of thick sour cream and one ounce or two cakes of yeast dissolved with a little sugar in two tablespoons of lukewarm milk. Stir all together and add three cups of flour; mix and drop from end of teaspoon on well-greased pans. Let rise until light in a warm place. Place a raisin or cherry on the top of each cake, spread with beaten white of egg, sprinkle with sugar and bake ten minutes in a hot oven.

RUSSIAN TEA CAKES

Mix one cup of sugar, one cup of eggs (about five), and one cup of sour cream with enough flour to roll. Toss on board, roll out one-fourth inch thick, spread with a thin layer of butter, fold the dough over, roll and spread again; repeat three or four times, using altogether three-fourths pound of brick butter. Then place dough in a bowl, cover, and let stand on ice to harden. Then roll as thin as possible, strew with one cup of chopped almonds, sugar and cinnamon, and cut into seven-inch strips. Roll each strip separately into a roll, cut into squares and strew top with chopped almonds, sugar and cinnamon. Bake in a hot oven.

WIENER KIPFEL

Dissolve one ounce of yeast in one-half cup of lukewarm milk, a pinch of salt and one tablespoon of sugar, set away in a warm place to rise. Sift one pound of flour into a deep bowl and make a dough of one cup of lukewarm milk and the yeast. Set it away until you have prepared the following: Rub a quarter of a pound of butter and four ounces of sugar to a cream, adding yolks of three eggs and one whole egg. Add this to the dough and work well. Let it rise about one hour, then roll out on a well-floured board, just as you would for cookies and let it rise again for at least one-half hour. Spread with beaten whites of eggs, raisins, almonds and citron. Cut dough into triangles. Pinch the edges together. Lay them in well-buttered pans about two inches apart and let then rise again. Then spread again with stiff-beaten whites of eggs and lay a few pounded almonds on each one. Bake a light yellow.

SPICE ROLL

Roll out coffee cake dough quite thin and let it rise half an hour, brush with melted butter and make a filling of the following: Grate some lebkuchen or plain gingerbread; add one-half cup of almonds or nuts, one cup of seeded raisins and one cup of cleaned currants. Strew these all over the dough together with some brown sugar and a little syrup. Spice with cinnamon and roll. Spread with butter and let it rise for an hour. Bake brown.

WIENER STUDENTEN KIPFEL

Make dough same as for Wiener Kipfel. Roll it out quite thin on a well-floured board and let it rise. Cut also into triangles (before you cut them, spread with melted butter). Mix one cup of chopped fresh walnuts with one cup of brown sugar, juice of a lemon, or grind the nuts; add cream to make a paste, sugar to taste and flavor with vanilla, and fill the triangles with the mixture. Take up the three corners and pinch together tightly. Set in well-buttered pans and let them rise again and spread or brush each one with melted butter. Bake a light brown.

YEAST KRANTZ

Take coffee cake dough, add one-fourth cup of washed currants. Let rise in warm place, then toss on floured board. Divide into three or four equal parts, roll each part into a long strand and work the strands together to form one large braid. Place braid in form of a circle in greased baking-pan or twist the braid to resemble the figure eight, pretzel shape. Let rise again in a warm place and bake in a moderate oven one-half hour or until thoroughly done. Brush with beaten eggs and sugar, sprinkle with a few chopped almonds. Return to oven to brown slightly.

STOLLEN

Sift two pounds of flour into a bowl and set a sponge in it with one cake of compressed yeast, one teaspoon of salt, one pint of lukewarm milk and one tablespoon of sugar. When this has risen, add one-half pound of creamed butter, a quarter of a pound of seeded raisins and one-quarter of a pound of sugar, yolks of four eggs, four ounces of powdered almonds, and the grated peel of a lemon. Work all well, beating with the hands, not kneading. Let this dough rise at least three hours, roll, press down the centre and fold over double, then form into one or two long loaves, narrow at the end. Brush the top with melted butter, let rise again and bake three-quarters of an hour in a moderate oven.

APPLE CAKE (KUCHEN)

After the pan is greased with butter, roll out a piece of dough quite thin, lay it in the pan, press a rim out of the dough all around the pan and let it rise for about ten minutes. Pare five large apples, core and quarter them, dipping each piece in melted butter before laying on the cake, sprinkle bountifully with sugar (brown being preferable to white for this purpose) and cinnamon. See that you have tart apples. Leave the cake in the pans and cut out the pieces just as you would want to serve them. If they stick to the pan, set the pan on top of the hot stove for a minute and the cake will then come out.

CHEESE CAKE OR PIE

Take one and one-half cups of cheese, rub smooth with a silver or wooden spoon through a colander or sieve, then rub a piece of sweet butter the size of an egg to a cream, add gradually one-half cup of sugar and the yolks of three eggs, a pinch of salt, grate in the peel of a lemon, one-half cup of cleaned currants and a little citron cut up very fine. Line two pie-plates with some kuchen dough or pie dough (See "Coffee Cakes (Kuchen)"), roll it out quite thin, butter the pie-plates quite heavily, and let the dough in them rise at least a quarter of an hour before putting in the cheese mixture, for it must be baked immediately after the cheese is put in, and just before you put the cheese into the plates whip up the whites of the eggs to a very stiff froth and stir through the cheese mixture.

CHERRY CAKE

Line a cake-pan, which has been well-buttered, with a thin layer of kuchen dough. Stone two pounds of cherries and lay them on a sieve with a dish underneath to catch the juice. Sprinkle sugar over them and bake. In the meantime beat up four eggs with a cup of sugar, beat until light and add the cherry juice. Draw the kuchen to the oven door, pour this mixture over it and bake.

PEACH KUCHEN

Grease your cake-pans thoroughly with good clarified butter, then line them with a rich coffee cake dough which has been rolled very thin and set in a warm place to rise. Then pare and quarter enough peaches to cover the dough. Lay the peaches in rows and sweeten and set in oven to bake. Make a meringue quickly as possible and pour over the cakes and bake a light brown.

FRESH PRUNE CAKE (KUCHEN)

Line a greased biscuit-pan with some of the coffee cake dough. Roll the dough thin and let it come up on the sides of the pan, then set aside to rise. When risen, cut the prunes in halves (they must be the fresh ones, not dried), lay in rows thickly and close together all over the bottom of the pan, do not leave any space between the prunes. Sprinkle very thickly with sugar, lightly with cinnamon, and lay bits of fresh butter all over the top. Bake until done in a moderately hot oven.

PRUNE CAKE (KUCHEN)

Line one or two plates with a thin roll of kuchen dough and let it rise again in the pans which have been heavily greased. Have some prunes boiled very soft, take out the kernels, mash them until like mush, sweeten to taste, add cinnamon and grated peel of a lemon or lemon juice, put in the lined pie-plates and bake immediately. Serve with whipped cream, sweetened and flavored.

HUCKLEBERRY KUCHEN

Line your cake-pans, which should be long and narrow, with a rich kuchen dough, having previously greased them well. Make a paste of cornstarch, one cup of milk, one tablespoon of butter and one teaspoon of cornstarch wet with cold milk. Boil until thick, sweeten and flavor with vanilla and spread on top of the cake dough, then sprinkle thickly with huckleberries which have been carefully picked, sugared and sprinkled with ground cinnamon. Bake in a quick oven.

HUCKLEBERRY PIE

Clean, pick and wash two cups of huckleberries, then drain them. Beat yolk of one egg and two tablespoons of sugar until light, add one tablespoon of milk, then the drained berries. Line one pie-plate with rich pastry or cookie dough, pour on it the berry mixture, put in the oven and bake light brown;

remove from the oven, spread with a meringue made of the white of the egg beaten stiff, and two tablespoons of sugar added. Brown nicely. The white can be beaten with the yolk and sugar, if preferred.

MUFFINS AND BISCUITS

BAKING-POWDER

Put eight ounces of bicarbonate of soda, one ounce of tartaric acid and one package of high-grade cornstarch together and sift them thoroughly five times. Keep closely covered in glass jars or tin boxes.

BAKING-POWDER BATTERS

Batter is a mixture of flour with sufficient liquid to make it thin enough to be beaten.

Pour-batter requires one measure of liquid to one measure of flour.

Drop-batter requires one measure of liquid to two measures of flour.

To make a batter. Sift flour before measuring. Put flour by spoonfuls into the cup; do not press or shake down. Mix and sift dry ingredients. Measure dry, then liquid ingredients, shortening may be rubbed or chopped in while cold, or creamed; or it may be melted and then added to dry ingredients, or added after the liquid. Use two teaspoons of baking-powder to one cup of flour. If eggs are used, less baking-powder will be required.

When sour milk is used, take one level teaspoon of soda to a pint of milk; when molasses is used, take one teaspoon of soda or baking-powder to each cup of molasses.

Mix dry materials in one bowl and liquids in another, combine them quickly, handle as little as possible and put at once into the oven.

The oven for baking biscuits should be hot enough to brown a teaspoon of flour in one minute.

BROWN BREAD

Mix and sift together one cup each of rye, graham flour, corn-meal and one teaspoon of salt. Dissolve one teaspoon of soda in one cup of molasses. Add alternately to flour with two cups of sour milk. Grease one-pound baking-powder cans, put in the dough and boil two and one-half hours, keeping the water always three-fourths up around the tins. Turn out on baking-tins and place in the oven fifteen minutes to brown.

To be eaten warm, whatever is left over can be steamed again or toasted.

CORN BREAD

Mix and sift one cup of corn-meal, one cup of flour, two tablespoons of sugar, one-half teaspoon of salt, three teaspoons of baking-powder. Melt one tablespoon of butter and add to one egg; mix milk and egg and beat this into the dry ingredients, pour this mixture into well-greased tins and bake in a hot oven one-half hour. Cut in squares and serve hot. Bake in gem tins if preferred.

BRAN BREAD

Sift four teaspoons of soda, two teaspoons of salt with four cups of white flour, add four cups of bran flour and mix well. Add one cup of molasses and four cups of sweet milk. Use chopped nuts or raisins or both as desired. This will make three or four flat loaves. Place in greased pans (four and a half by nine inches), and bake one hour in a moderate oven.

JOHNNIE CAKE

Mix one cup flour and two cups corn-meal, one heaping teaspoon of soda, one-half cup sugar, add two eggs beaten with one and one-half cups of buttermilk, one half cup of molasses and one-half cup of shortening, melted. Beat all ingredients as fast as possible for a minute. Pour the dough into a warm, well-buttered pan and bake quickly and steadily for half an hour. The dough should be as soft as gingerbread dough. Serve hot.

EGGLESS GINGERBREAD WITH CHEESE

Sift two cups of flour, one teaspoon of soda, one-half teaspoon of salt and two teaspoons of ginger. Melt three-fourths cup of grated cheese in one-half cup of hot water, add one-half cup of molasses and blend perfectly. Add the flour and seasonings very gradually and beat thoroughly. Bake in muffin rings for fifteen minutes and serve while warm.

GINGERBREAD

To one cup of molasses add one cup of milk, sour or sweet, dissolve one teaspoon of soda in the milk, one tablespoon of butter, one or two eggs, one teaspoon of ginger and one of ground cinnamon, add enough sifted flour to make a light batter. Bake in a shallow pan.

WHITE NUT BREAD

Mix two and one-half cups of flour, four teaspoons of baking-powder, one-half teaspoon of salt, one-half cup of sugar and one-half cup of walnut meats, broken; add one egg beaten with one cup of milk and let this mixture stand for about twenty minutes in well-greased breadpan before placing in a moderate oven to bake. Bake about an hour. Better day after it is made.

BAKING-POWDER BISCUITS

Sift two cups of flour with one-half teaspoon of salt, four teaspoons of baking-powder, and four tablespoons of butter; cut butter in with two knives and mix with one-half to two-thirds cup of water or milk, stir this in quickly with a knife, when well mixed place on a well-floured board and roll out about one inch thick, work quickly, cut with a biscuit cutter or the cover of a half-pound baking-powder can; place on a greased pan and bake quickly in a well-heated quick oven tea to fifteen minutes.

Butter substitutes may be used in place of butter.

DROP BISCUIT

Add to ingredients for baking-powder biscuit enough more milk or water to make a thick drop batter, about two tablespoons; mix as directed for biscuit, drop by spoonfuls an inch apart on a greased baking-sheet or into greased gem pans, small size.

The more crust the more palatable these biscuits are. The mixture should not be soft enough to run. Bake in a hot oven ten to twelve minutes.

SOUR MILK BISCUITS

Mix and sift two cups of flour, one-half teaspoon of salt and one-half teaspoon of soda; cut in one tablespoon of butter, stir in with a knife enough sour milk to make a soft dough. Roll one-half inch thick; cut in small rounds and bake in a quick oven about twenty minutes.

MUFFINS.

Light the burners of the gas oven before beginning to mix the muffins and work rapidly. Place in a mixing-bowl one well-beaten egg, two tablespoons of butter, one tablespoon of sugar, one-half teaspoon of salt, one scant cup of milk and two teaspoons of baking-powder that have been sifted with sufficient flour to form a batter that will "ribbon" from the spoon. Beat the batter steadily for five minutes, stir in one tablespoon of melted butter and bake in muffin-pans in a quick oven. These muffins will bake in ten minutes if pans are only half filled.

BRAN MUFFINS

Sift one-half cup of white flour with one teaspoon of soda; mix three tablespoons of molasses with one tablespoon of butter, add two cups of bran, one and one-half cups of sweet milk, then add the flour and one-half teaspoon of salt, stir all together; one-half cup of chopped dates or raisins may be added if so desired. Bake in muffin-pans in a moderate oven thirty minutes.

CORN MUFFINS, No. 1

Beat the yolks and whites of two eggs separately. Add to this two cups of flour, of which one is a full cup of white and three-quarters of the corn-meal. This must be sifted three times. Put into this flour two teaspoons of baking-powder, together with a pinch of salt. Mix the prepared flour with a little boiling water, adding the eggs; also a little sugar may be put in, if desired. Then add enough tepid milk to make the mixture into a batter, after which pour into your pans; or, if corn-bread is desired, into the plain pan (thin). Bake in a quick oven. This quantity makes a dozen muffins. Butter your pan well, or the small gem-pans, according to which is used, and in so doing heat the pan a little.

CORN MUFFINS, No. 2

Mix one cup of white flour; one-half cup of corn-meal, one tablespoon of sugar, one-half teaspoon of salt and one-half teaspoon of soda, add one egg beaten into one cup of sour milk and one tablespoon of melted butter. Beat thoroughly and bake in well-greased tins.

GRAHAM MUFFINS

Mix one cup of Graham flour, one cup of wheat flour, one-half teaspoon of salt, two teaspoons of baking-powder, add to this one tablespoon of melted butter creamed with one-half cup of sugar and one well-beaten egg, moisten with one and one-half cups of milk. Beat all well and bake in muffin-tins in moderately hot oven one-half hour.

WHEAT MUFFINS

Mix two cups of flour, one-half teaspoon of salt, three teaspoons of baking-powder, two tablespoons of sugar and sift these ingredients twice, rub in one tablespoon of butter. Separate one egg. Beat the yolk and add it to one cup of milk and one teaspoon of molasses. Mix with the dry ingredients and stir until smooth. Fold in the beaten white of egg and pour into hot, well-greased muffin-tins. Bake fifteen to twenty minutes in hot oven.

RICE MUFFINS

Beat one cup of cold rice, two eggs, one cup of sweet milk, one teaspoon of salt, one tablespoon of sugar, two teaspoons of baking-powder, enough flour to make a stiff batter and lastly one tablespoon of melted butter. Bake in muffin-tins.

RYE FLOUR MUFFINS

Sift one and one-half cups of rye flour with one-half teaspoon of salt and one teaspoon of baking soda; add one-half cup of molasses and one well-beaten egg or one-half cup of water if the egg is omitted, one-quarter cup of chopped raisins and four tablespoons of melted shortening—butter, or any good butter substitute will do. Bake in muffin-pans in rather hot oven twenty-five minutes. Fill pans three-fourths full.

GLUTEN GEMS

Beat the yolks of two eggs, add one cup of milk; then one and one-half cups of gluten flour, two teaspoons of baking powder; beat well, stir in the whites of the two eggs, and bake in hot buttered gem pans about twenty minutes.

EGGLESS GINGER GEMS

Mix one-half cup of molasses, one-half cup of sugar, one tablespoon of butter, and warm slightly; beat up well and stir at least ten minutes. Add the following spices: one-half teaspoon each of ginger and cinnamon; and gradually one-half cup of milk and two and one-half cups of sifted flour in which has been sifted two teaspoons of baking powder. One-fourth cup of currants or seeded raisins may be added. Bake in well-greased gem pans and eat warm for tea or lunch.

POPOVERS

Mix to a smooth batter two cups each of milk and well-sifted flour, the yolks of three fresh eggs and a teaspoon of salt. Butter well the inside of six or eight deep earthen popover cups and stand them in a pan in a hot oven. While the cups are heating, beat to a froth the whites of the three eggs and stir them quickly in the batter. Open the oven door, pull the pan forward, pour the batter in the hot buttered cups up to the brim. Push the pan back, close the oven door, and bake the popovers till they rise well and are brown at the sides where they part from the clips. Serve them hot, folded lightly in a napkin.

ONE-EGG WAFFLES

Mix one and one-half cups of flour, one teaspoon of baking powder, one-quarter teaspoon of salt; add one and three-fourths cups of milk, add the milk slowly; then one well-beaten egg and two tablespoons of melted butter; drop by spoonfuls on a hot buttered waffle iron, putting one tablespoon in each section of the iron. Bake and turn, browning both sides carefully; remove from the iron; pile one on top of the other and serve at once.

THREE-EGG WAFFLES

Mix two cups of flour, one teaspoon of baking-powder, one-half teaspoon of salt, and sift these ingredients; add the yolks of three eggs beaten and stirred into one and one-fourth cups of milk; then add one tablespoon of melted butter and fold in the whites of the eggs. Bake and serve as directed under One-Egg Waffles.

DOUGHNUTS

Mix two and one-half tablespoons of melted butter, one cup of granulated sugar, two eggs, one cup of milk, one-half nutmeg grated, sifted flour enough to make a batter as stiff as biscuit dough; add two teaspoons of baking-powder and one teaspoon of salt to the sifted flour. Flour your board well, roll dough out about half an inch thick, and cut into pieces three inches long and one inch wide. Cut a slit about an inch long in the centre of each strip and pull one end through this slit. Fry quickly in hot Crisco. Sprinkle powdered sugar on top of each doughnut.

FRENCH DOUGHNUTS

French doughnuts are much daintier than the ordinary ones, and are easily made. Take one-half pint of water, one-half pint of milk, six ounces of butter, one-half pound of flour, and six eggs. Heat the butter, milk, and water, and when it boils remove from the fire and stir in the flour, using a wooden spoon. When well mixed, stir in the eggs, whipping each one in separately until you have a hard batter. Now pour your dough into a pastry bag. This is an ordinary cheesecloth bag, one corner of which has a tiny tin funnel, with a fluted or fancy edge. (These little tins may be purchased at any tinware store.) It should be very small, not over two inches high at the most, so the dough may be easily squeezed through it. Pour the paste on buttered paper, making into ring shapes. Fry in hot oil or butter substitute. Dust with powdered sugar.

CRULLERS

Cream two tablespoons of butter with one-half cup of sugar, then beat in one at a time two whole eggs. Mix well, then add one-half cup of milk, two teaspoons of baking-powder, and sufficient flour to make a soft batter to roll out. (Try three cupfuls and then add as much more flour as necessary.) Last, add one-half teaspoon cinnamon. Roll one-half inch thick, cut in strips one inch wide, three inches long and fry in hot Crisco.

STRAWBERRY SHORTCAKE (BISCUIT DOUGH)

Mix two cups of flour, four teaspoons of baking-powder, one-half teaspoon of salt, one tablespoon of sugar; work one-quarter cup of butter with tips of fingers, and add three-quarters of a cup of milk gradually. Toss on floured board, divide in two parts. Pat, roll out and bake twelve minutes in hot oven in layer-cake tins. Split and spread with butter. Pick, hull, and drain berries. Sweeten one to one and one-half boxes of strawberries to taste. Crush slightly and put between and on top of short cake. Allow from one to one and one-half boxes of berries to each short cake. Serve with cream, plain or whipped.

Strawberries make the best short cake, but other berries and sliced peaches are also good.

DOUGH FOR OPEN FACE PIES

The directions for making the dough for Cinnamon Buns may be followed in making the under crust for fruit pies, such as apple, plum, huckleberry and peach.

Enough for two pies. Drippings and water may be substituted for butter and milk respectively.

CINNAMON BUNS

Sift together one pint of flour, one tablespoon of sugar, one-half teaspoon of salt, two teaspoons of baking-powder. Rub in two tablespoons of butter, mix with milk to soft dough. Roll out one-half inch thick, spread with soft butter, granulated sugar, and powdered cinnamon. Roll up like jelly roll, cut in inch slices, lay close together in greased pan, and bake in quick oven.

FRUIT WHEELS

Sift together two cups of flour, two teaspoons of baking-powder, one-half teaspoon of salt, one tablespoon of sugar. Rub in two large tablespoons of butter. Mix to soft dough with milk; roll out one-half inch thick. Spread thickly with soft butter, dust with one teaspoon of flour, four tablespoons of granulated sugar, one teaspoon of cinnamon; sprinkle over one-half cup each of seeded and cut raisins, chopped citron, and cleaned currants. Roll up, cut in one-inch slices, put one inch apart on greased, flat pans, and bake in hot oven.

PANCAKES, FRITTERS, Etc.

BUCKWHEAT CAKES

Dissolve one cake of compressed yeast and two level teaspoons of brown sugar in two cups of lukewarm water and one cup of milk, scalded and cooled; add two cups of buckwheat and one cup of sifted white flour gradually and one and one-half teaspoons of salt. Beat until smooth; cover and set aside in a warm place, free from draft, to rise about one hour. When light stir well and bake on a hot griddle. If wanted for overnight, use only one-fourth cake of yeast and an extra half teaspoon of salt. Cover and keep in a cool place.

GERMAN PANCAKES, No. 1

Beat two eggs very thoroughly without separating the yolks and whites; add one-half teaspoon of salt, sift in two and one-half tablespoons of flour, add one cup of milk gradually at first, and beat the whole very well. Melt one tablespoon of butter in a large frying-pan, turn mixture in and cook slowly until brown underneath. Grease the bottom of a large pie plate, slip the pancake on the plate; add the other tablespoon of butter to the frying-pan; when hot, turn uncooked side of pancake down and brown. Serve at once with sugar and lemon slices or with any desired preserve or syrup. This pancake may be served rolled like a jelly roll.

GERMAN PANCAKES, No. 2

Beat two eggs until very light, add one-half cup of flour and one-half teaspoon of salt and beat again; then add one cup of milk slowly, and beat thoroughly. Heat a generous quantity of butter in a frying-pan and pour all the batter into this at one time; place on a hot stove for one minute; then remove to a brisk oven; the edges will turn up on sides of pan in a few minutes; then reduce heat and cook more slowly until light, crisp and brown, about seven minutes. Take it out, slide it carefully on a hot plate, sprinkle plentifully with powdered sugar and send to the table with six lemon slices.

GERMAN PANCAKES, No. 3

Beat the yolks of four eggs until very light, then add one-half cup of milk and stir in three-quarters cup of sifted flour, one-eighth teaspoon of baking-powder, a pinch of salt, and lastly, just before frying, add the stiffly-beaten whites of eggs and mix well together. Put on fire an iron skillet with a close-fitting top; heat in two tablespoons of rendered butter; when very hot, pour in enough of the batter to cover the bottom of the skillet, cover at once with the top, and when the pancake is brown on one side, remove the top and let it brown on the other side. Take it up with a perforated skimmer, lay on a plate and sprinkle with powdered sugar and some lemon juice. Serve at once. Pancakes must only be made and fried when ready to be eaten, as they fall from standing.

BREAD PANCAKES

Soak stale bread overnight in sour milk, mash the bread fine in the morning, and put in one-half teaspoon of salt, two eggs, two teaspoons of baking soda, dissolved in hot water, and thicken with finely sifted flour.

RICE PANCAKES OR GRIDDLE CAKES

Boil in a double boiler one pint of milk, three tablespoons of rice and two tablespoons of granulated sugar. It will take from fifty to sixty minutes for the rice to be thoroughly cooked, and the mixture to thicken. Remove from the fire and when a little cool, add one tablespoon of vanilla and the yolk of egg into which one tablespoon of flour has been smoothly stirred. Mix all thoroughly together, then pour, by spoonfuls, on hot buttered griddle. Let the cakes brown on one side, and turn over, and brown on the other.

GRIMSLICH

Half a loaf of bread, which has been soaked and pressed, two eggs; one-half cup of sugar, one-fourth cup raisins, one tablespoon of cinnamon, and one-fourth cup of almonds pounded fine. Beat whites to a froth and add last. Drop by tablespoonful and fry. Serve with stewed fruit. Pieces of stale bread can be used. Soak in tepid water. Squeeze water thoroughly from bread and make as directed.

POTATO PANCAKES

Peel six large potatoes and soak several hours in cold water; grate, drain, and for every pint allow two eggs, about one tablespoon of flour, one-half teaspoon of salt, a little pepper; a little onion juice may be added if so desired. Beat eggs well and mix with the rest of the ingredients. Drop by spoonfuls on a hot greased spider in small cakes. Turn and brown on both sides. Serve with apple sauce.

When eggs are very expensive the cakes can be made with one egg. When required for a meat meal, the pancakes may be fried in drippings; the edges will be much more crisp than when fried in butter, which burns so readily.

POTATO CAKES

Made just as pancakes, only baked in the oven in a long cake pan with plenty of butter or drippings under and above.

SOUR MILK PANCAKES

Mash fine and dissolve one level teaspoon of baking-soda in three cups of sour milk; beat one egg well; then put in a little salt and one-half cup of flour; stir in the milk, make a smooth batter, and last stir in one tablespoon of syrup. Bake on a hot griddle.

FRENCH PANCAKE

Stir three egg-yolks with one-half teaspoon of salt and one-quarter cup of flour, until smooth; add one cup of cold milk gradually, then fold in the beaten whites. Heat pan, add two tablespoons of butter and when hot pour in pancake; let cook slowly and evenly on one side, finish baking in oven.

CHEESE BLINTZES

With a fork beat up one egg, one-half teaspoon of salt, add one cup of water and one cup of sifted flour, beat until smooth. Grease a frying-pan very slightly with butter or oil, pour in two tablespoons of the batter, tilting the pan so as to allow the batter to run all over the pan. Fry over a low heat on one side only, turn out the semi-cooked cakes on a clean cloth with the uncooked side uppermost; let cool. Prepare a filling as for cheese kreplich, using one-half pound of potcheese, a piece of butter size of an egg, add one egg, pinch of salt, a little cinnamon and sugar to taste and grated peel of a lemon. Spread this mixture on the cooled dough, fold over and tuck the edges in well. Then sprinkle with powdered sugar and cinnamon, and fry in plenty of oil or butter. These blintzes are served hot.

SWEET BLINTZES

These little pancakes may be filled with the fruit filling in following recipe; or with a poppy seed filling using one cup of seed and adding one cup of sugar, moistening with one-half cup of water. The recipe given for the dough makes only six blintzes and where more are required double or triple the quantities given to make amount desired.

For Purim, fold blintzes in triangular shapes. Fry as directed.

BLINTZES

Make dough as directed for cheese blintzes. Filling may be made of force meat, highly seasoned; fry in hot fat, or filling may be made of one-half pound of apples, peeled and cored and then minced with one ounce of ground sweet almonds, one ounce of powdered sugar, a pinch of cinnamon, juice of one-half lemon; mix well and bind with the beaten white of egg.

Spread either of these mixtures on the dough, fold over and tuck edges in well. Fry in plenty of oil or fat.

Sprinkle those containing the fruit mixture with sugar and cinnamon. These may be served either hot or cold.

FRITTER BATTER

Mix and sift one and one-third cups of flour, two teaspoons of baking-powder, one-quarter teaspoon of salt, and add two-thirds cup of milk or water gradually, and one egg; well beaten. For fruit batter add a little sugar, for vegetables pepper and salt.

BELL FRITTERS

Stir three eggs until very light, then stir in one cup of sweet milk, then sift in three cups sifted flour; beat for ten minutes, then add three teaspoons of baking-powder and fry by spoonfuls in hot oil. One-half this amount will be sufficient for three persons.

Serve with any sweet sauce.

APPLE FRITTERS

Choose four sour apples; pare, core and cut them into small slices. Stir into fritter batter and fry in boiling hot fat or oil. Drain on paper; sprinkle with powdered sugar and serve.

PINEAPPLE FRITTERS

Soak slices of pineapple in sherry or white wine with a little sugar and let stand one hour. Drain and dip slices in batter and fry in hot oil. Drain on brown paper and sprinkle with powdered sugar.

Fresh pears, apricots and peach fritters made the same as pineapple fritters. Bananas are cut in slices or mashed and added to batter.

ORANGE FRITTERS

Yolks of two eggs beaten with two spoons of sugar, stir into this the juice of quarter of a lemon and just enough flour to thicken like a batter; add the beaten whites and dip in one slice of orange at a time, take up with a large kitchen spoon and lay in the hot oil or butter-substitute and fry a nice brown. Sprinkle pulverized sugar on top.

MATRIMONIES

Sift three cups of flour in a bowl, pour in two scant cups of sour milk, beat very thoroughly, add one teaspoon of salt, the well-beaten yolks of three eggs, mix well, then add the stiffly-beaten whites of the eggs and one level teaspoon of soda sifted with one teaspoon of flour. Mix well and fry at once in very hot butter or butter-substitute. Baste the grease over them with a spoon until they are nicely browned. Serve with preserves.

QUEEN FRITTERS

Put in a deep skillet on the fire one cup of water, one-fourth cup of fresh butter; when it comes to a boil, stir in one cup of sifted flour and continue stirring until the dough leaves the side of the skillet clean. Remove from the fire and when cool break in three eggs, one at a time, stirring continually. Add a little salt. Mix all well, then drop pieces about the size of a walnut into plenty of boiling butter or Crisco and fry a light brown. Drain, make an opening in each, fill with preserves and sprinkle with sugar; serve at once.

VEGETABLE FRITTERS

Cook the vegetables thoroughly; drain them, chop fine and add to the batter. Drop in boiling hot fat, drain and dry on paper.

CORN FRITTERS

Grate two cups of corn from the cob. Ears that are too old for eating in the ordinary method will serve very well for this. Mix with the corn one egg, beaten light, a cup of sweet milk into which has been stirred a bit of soda the size of a pea, two teaspoons of melted butter, a pinch of salt and enough flour to make a thin batter. Beat well together and fry on a griddle as you would cakes for breakfast.

ERBSEN LIEVANZEN (DRIED PEA FRITTERS)

Boil one cup of dried peas, pass through a hair sieve, pour into a bowl, add two ounces of butter rubbed to a cream, add also some soaked bread (soaked in milk), stir all into a smooth paste. Add salt, one teaspoon of sugar, one yolk and one whole egg; one ounce of blanched and pounded almonds. If too thick add more egg, if too thin more bread. Fry a nice brown.

SQUASH FRITTERS

Two cups of boiled squash, half a cup of flour, one teaspoon of baking-powder, one egg and two tablespoons of milk. It is assumed that the squash has been prepared as a vegetable, with seasoning and a little butter, and what is here used is a cold, left over portion of the same. Mix baking-powder with the flour and add to the squash; add milk and stir all together. Beat egg and stir in. Have hot fat in pan and drop fritters from spoon into pan. When browned on both sides remove to hot platter.

FRENCH PUFFS (WINDBEUTEL)

Put one cup of water and one-quarter pound of butter on to boil. When it begins to boil stir in one-quarter pound of sifted flour. Stir until it leaves the kettle clean, take off the fire and stir until milk-warm, then stir in four eggs, one at a time, stirring until all used up. Flavor with the grated peel of a lemon. Put on some rendered butter in a kettle. When the butter is hot, dip a large teaspoon in cold water and cut pieces of dough with it as large as a walnut, and drop into the hot butter. Try one first to see whether the butter is hot enough. Do not crowd—they want plenty of room to raise. Dip the hot butter over them with a spoon, fry a deep yellow and sprinkle powdered sugar over them.

SHAVINGS (KRAUS-GEBACKENES)

Sift about one pint of flour in a bowl, make a depression in the centre; break in five eggs, a pinch of salt, one teaspoon of ground cinnamon and one tablespoon of pulverized sugar. Mix this as you would a noodle dough, though not quite as stiff. Roll out very thin and cut into long strips with a jagging iron. Fry a light yellow. Roll on a round stick as soon as taken up from the fat or butter, sprinkle with sugar and cinnamon or grated peel of a lemon. Mix both thoroughly. Do not let the butter get too brown; if the fire is too strong take off a few minutes.

SNIP NOODLES, FRIED

Sift two cups of flour with three teaspoons of salt in it, make into a dough by adding enough sweet milk to make soft as biscuit dough. Break off small pieces and roll between the hands in the shape of croquettes.

Now put one-half cup of rendered butter in a skillet that has a top to it; when the butter is hot, lay in the pieces of dough (do not put too many in at one time), throw in one-half cup of cold water, put on the cover and let cook until the water is cooked out and noodles are brown on one side. Remove the cover and brown on the other side.

NOODLE PUFFS

Make a noodle dough with as many eggs as desired, roll out somewhat thin, cut in strips four inches long by one inch wide.

Have a skillet half full of boiling hot chicken fat; drop in the strips, a few at a time, baste with the hot grease until brown on both sides. Remove to a platter, sprinkle generously with powdered sugar and cinnamon, and serve.

SNOWBALLS (HESTERLISTE)

Mix one teaspoon of butter, one-fourth teaspoon of salt, one tablespoon of sugar with one egg. Add one tablespoon of cream, one teaspoon of brandy and flour to make stiff dough. Work the whole together with a spoon until the flour is incorporated with the other ingredients and you have a dough easily handled. Break the dough in pieces about the size of a walnut; roll each piece out separately just as thin as possible without tearing (the thinner the better), make three lengthwise slashes in the centre of each piece of dough after rolling out.

Heat a large deep skillet about half full with boiling hot butter or Crisco, drop in the snowballs, not more than three at one time, brown quickly on one side, then on the other, turn carefully with a perforated skimmer as they are easily broken. Remove to a platter, sprinkle with powdered sugar and cinnamon and a few drops of lemon juice.

CAKES

GENERAL DIRECTIONS FOR MAKING CAKES

Use only the best material in making cake.

Gather together all ingredients and utensils that are required. If tins are to be greased, do so the first thing; some cakes require greased or buttered paper, if so, have paper cut the size that is needed and butter the paper.

All measurements are level. See "Measurement of Food Materials".

Use pastry flour. Sift flour twice at least and measure after sifting.

Measure or weigh the sugar, butter, milk and flour. In measuring butter always pack the cup so as to be sure to get the proper quantity. Use the half-pint measuring cup.

If fruit is to be used, wash and dry it the day before it is needed. Dust with flour just before using, and mix with the hand till each piece is powdered so that all will mix evenly with the dough instead of sinking to the bottom.

A few necessary implements for good cake making are a pair of scales, a wooden spoon, two wire egg-whips, one for the yolks and the other for the whites of eggs.

A ten-inch mixing-bowl, and two smaller bowls.

Two spatula or leveling knives.

A set of aluminum spoons of standard sizes.

For convenience, cakes are divided into two classes: Those containing butter or a butter substitute and cake containing no shortening.

The rules for mixing cakes with butter are:

Break the eggs, dropping each in a saucer or cup. If the whites and yolks are to be used separately divide them as you break the eggs and beat both well before using; the yolks until light and the whites to a stiff froth, so stiff that you can turn the dish upside down and the eggs will adhere to the dish.

Rub the butter to a cream which should be done with a wooden spoon in a deep bowl, add the sugar gradually. In winter set the bowl over hot water for a few minutes as the butter will then cream more easily. Add the yolks or the whole eggs, one at a time, to creamed butter and sugar. Sift the baking-powder with the last cup of flour, add flour and milk alternately until both are beaten thoroughly into the mixture, add beaten whites of eggs last to the dough and then set in the oven immediately.

Sponge cakes and cakes that do not contain butter and milk must never be stirred, but the ingredients beaten in, being careful to beat with an upward stroke. Separate the yolks of the eggs from the whites, and beat the yolks with an egg-beater until they are thick and lemon-colored. Then add the sugar, a little at a time, beating constantly. Now beat the whites until they are stiff and dry; add them; the flour should be added last and folded lightly through. Every stroke of the spoon after flour is added tends to toughen the batter. Bake at once. All sponge cakes and torten should be baked in ungreased molds.

TO BAKE CAKES

Make sure the oven is in condition, it can better wait for the cake than the other way around.

Light your gas oven five or ten minutes before needed and reduce heat accordingly when cake is put in oven.

For the coal range, have the oven the right temperature and do not add coal or shake the coals while cake is baking.

If a piece of soft yellow paper burns golden brown in five minutes the oven is moderately hot; if it takes four minutes the oven is hot, if seven minutes is required the oven is fit for slow baking.

Sponge cakes require a slow oven; layer cakes a hot oven, and loaf cakes with butter a moderate oven.

Never look after your cake until it has been in the oven ten minutes.

If cake is put in too cool an oven it will rise too much and be of very coarse texture. If too hot, it browns and crusts over the top before it has sufficiently risen. If, after the cake is put in, it seems to bake too fast, put a brown paper loosely over the top of the pan, and do not open the oven door for five minutes at least; the cake should then be quickly examined and the door carefully shut, or the rush of cold air will cause it to fall. Setting a small dish of hot water in the oven will also prevent the cake from scorching.

When you think your cake is baked, open the oven door carefully so as not to jar, take a straw and run it through the thickest part of the cake, and if the straw comes out perfectly clean and dry your cake is done. When done, take it out and set it where no draft of air will strike it, and in ten minutes turn it out on a flat plate or board.

Do not put it in the cake box until perfectly cold. Scald out the tin cake box each time before putting a fresh cake in it. Make sure it is air-tight. Keep in a cool place, but not in a damp cellar or a refrigerator.

TIME-TABLE FOR BAKING CAKES

Sponge cake, three-quarters of an hour.
Pound cake, one hour.
Fruit cake, three and four hours, depending upon size.
Cookies, from ten to fifteen minutes. Watch carefully.
Cup cakes, a full half hour.
Layer cakes, twenty minutes.

ONE EGG CAKE

Cream one-fourth cup of butter with one-half cup of sugar, add sugar gradually, and one egg, well-beaten. Mix and sift one and one-half cups of flour and two and one-half teaspoons of baking-powder, add the sifted flour alternately with one-half cup of milk to the first mixture; flavor with vanilla or lemon. Bake thirty minutes in a shallow pan. Spread with chocolate frosting.

LITTLE FRENCH CAKES

Beat one-fourth cup of butter to a cream with one-fourth cup of sugar and add one cup of flour. Stir well and then add one egg which has been beaten into half a pint of milk, a little at a time. Fill buttered saucers with the mixture, bake and when done, place the cakes one on top of another with jam spread between.

GRAFTON CAKE. LAYERS AND SMALL CAKES

Cream four tablespoons of butter with one and one-half cups of sugar, beat in separately two whole eggs, add one cup of milk alternately with two cups of flour in which has been sifted two teaspoons of baking-powder, beat all thoroughly.

This recipe will make two layer-cakes which may be spread with any of the cake fillings or icings.

To make small cakes omit one of the egg-whites, fill well-buttered gem pans a little more than half full, and bake in a moderately hot oven until a delicate brown. The white reserved may be beaten to a stiff froth and then gradually stir in four tablespoons of powdered sugar and the juice of half a lemon. When the cakes are cool, spread with the icing and decorate with raisins, nut meats, one on top of each or sprinkle with candied caraway seeds.

CUP CAKE

Cream one cup of butter with two cups of sugar and add gradually the yolks of four eggs, one at a time. Sift three cups of flour, measure again after sifting, and add two teaspoons of baking-powder in the last sifting. Add alternately the sifted flour and one cup of sweet milk. Add last the beaten whites of the eggs. Flavor to taste. Bake in loaf or jelly-tins.

GOLD CAKE

Take one cup of powdered sugar, one-half cup of butter rubbed to a cream; add yolks of six eggs and stir until very light. Then sift two cups of flour with one and one-half teaspoons of baking-powder sifted in well (sift the flour two or three times). Grate in the peel of a lemon or an orange, add the juice also, and add three-quarters cup of milk alternately with the flour. Bake in moderate oven.

WHITE CAKE

Cream three-quarters cup of butter and one and one-quarter cups of sugar very well. Stop stirring, pour one-half cup of cold water on top of butter mixture and whites of eight eggs slightly beaten on top of water; do not stir, add one teaspoon of vanilla. Sift two and one-half cups of pastry flour, measure, then mix with two heaping teaspoons of baking-powder, and sift three times. Add to cake mixture and then beat hard until very smooth. Turn into ungreased angel cake pan, place in slow oven. Let cake rise to top of pan, then increase heat and bake until firm. Invert pan, when cool cut out.

MARBLE CAKE

Take two cups of sugar, one cup of butter, four eggs (yolks), one cup of milk, three cups of flour, and three teaspoons of baking-powder (scant). Cream the butter and sugar, and add the yolks of eggs. Then add the milk, flour, baking-powder, and the beaten whites of the eggs; flavor with lemon. To make the brown part; take a square of bitter chocolate and melt above steam, and mix with some of the white; flavor the brown with vanilla. Put first a tablespoon of brown batter in the pan, and then the white. Bake in quick oven thirty-five minutes.

LEMON CAKE

Rub to a cream one-half cup of butter with one and one-half cups of pulverized sugar and add gradually the yolks of three eggs, one at a time, and one-half cup of sweet milk. Sift two cups of flour with one teaspoon of baking-powder, add alternately with the milk and the stiffly-beaten whites of three eggs. Add the grated peel of one-half lemon and the juice of one lemon. Bake in moderate oven thirty minutes.

ORANGE CAKE

Beat light the yolks of five eggs with two cups of pulverized sugar, add juice of a large orange and part of the peel grated; one-half a cup of cold water and two cups of flour, sifted three times. Add two teaspoons of baking-powder in last sifting and add last the stiff-beaten whites of three eggs. Bake in layers, and spread the following icing between and on top. Icing: beat the whites of two eggs stiff, add the juice and peel of one orange and sugar enough to stiffen.

POTATO CAKE

Cream two-thirds cup of butter with two cups of granulated sugar; add one-half cup of milk, yolks of four eggs, one cup of hot mashed potatoes, one cup of chocolate, one teaspoon each of cinnamon, cloves, and nutmeg, one teaspoon of vanilla, one cup of chopped walnuts, two cups of flour, two teaspoons of baking-powder, then beaten whites of four eggs. Bake slowly in two pans, and cut in half when cold. Put jam between layers.

POUND CAKE

Rub one pound of butter and one pound of powdered sugar to a cream, add the grated peel of a lemon, a glass of brandy and the yolks of nine eggs, added one at a time, and last one pound and a quarter of sifted flour with one-half teaspoon of baking-powder and the beaten whites of the eggs. Bake slowly.

BAKING-POWDER BUNT KUCHEN

Beat two whole eggs for ten minutes with two cups of sugar, two and one-half tablespoons of melted butter, add one cup of milk, three cups of flour in which have been sifted two teaspoons of baking-powder, flavor with one teaspoon of vanilla; one-fourth cup of small raisins may be added. Bake one hour.

QUICK COFFEE CAKE

Cream one-half cup of butter with one cup of sugar, add three eggs, one and one-half cups of flour, two teaspoons of baking-powder, mixed with the flour, and one-half cup of milk. Mix well together; bake in a long bread or cake pan, and have on top chopped almonds, sugar and cinnamon.

BAKING-POWDER CINNAMON CAKE

Cream three-fourths cup of sugar with a piece of butter the size of an egg, beat together; then add two eggs, one-half cup of milk (scant), one and one-half cups of flour, one teaspoon of vanilla and two teaspoons of baking-powder. Put cinnamon, flour, sugar and a few drops of water together and form in little pfärvel with your hand and sprinkle on top of cake; also sprinkle a few chopped nuts on top. Do not bake too quickly. Bake in flat pan.

GERMAN COFFEE CAKE (BAKING-POWDER)

Take three cups of flour sifted, one teaspoon of salt, three tablespoons of sugar, three teaspoons of baking-powder, two eggs, two tablespoons of butter, and two-thirds of a cup of milk. Stir well together, adding more milk if necessary. Keep batter very stiff, sprinkle with melted butter (generously) sugar and cinnamon, and again with melted butter. Put into well-buttered shallow pans and bake about half an hour.

COVERED CHEESE CAKE

Cream one cup of sugar with butter the size of an egg, add two eggs well beaten and one cup of water alternately with two and one-half cups of flour in which has been sifted two teaspoons of baking-powder.

Filling.—Beat two eggs with one-half cup of sugar, add one-half pound of pot cheese, one tablespoon of cornstarch boiled in one cup of milk, cool this and add, flavor with lemon extract.

Put one-half of the batter in cake pan, then the filling and the other half of batter. Bake in slow oven thirty-five minutes. Sift sugar on top when done.

BLITZ KUCHEN

Take one cup of powdered sugar, one-half cup of butter, one cup of pastry flour, one-quarter of a teaspoon of baking-powder, peel and juice of one lemon, five or six eggs. Beat sugar with two whole eggs; add butter, beat until foamy; after that the flour mixed with baking-powder, lemon and four yolks. Last the stiffly-beaten whites of the eggs. Mix this well, bake in form in a moderately hot oven.

KOENIG KUCHEN

Cream one-quarter cup of butter with one cup of sugar, yolks of six eggs, one-quarter pound of raisins, one-quarter pound of currants, juice and peel of one lemon, one spoon of rum, twenty blanched and grated almonds, two cups of flour mixed with one-half teaspoon of baking-powder, two stiffly-beaten whites of eggs. Bake in an ungreased form one to one and one-half hours.

NUT CAKE

Take one-half cup of butter, three eggs, one and one-half cups of sugar, two and one-half cups of flour, two and one-half level teaspoons of baking-powder, and one-half cup of milk. One cup of any kind of nuts. Rub the butter and sugar to a light white cream; add the eggs beaten a little; then the flour sifted with the powder. Mix with the milk and nuts into a rather firm batter. Bake in a paper lined tin in a steady oven thirty-five minutes.

LOAF COCOANUT CAKE

Rub one cup of butter and two cups of sugar to a cream. Add one cup of milk, whites of four eggs, three cups of flour (measure after sifting), and three teaspoons of baking-powder added in last sifting. Add a grated cocoanut and last the stiffly-beaten whites. Bake in a loaf. Line tin with buttered paper.

FRUIT CAKE (WEDDING CAKE)

Take one pound of butter and one pound of sugar rubbed to a cream, yolks of twelve eggs, one tablespoon of cinnamon, one teaspoon of allspice, one-half teaspoon of mace, one-half teaspoon of cloves, one-fourth of a pound of almonds pounded, two pounds of raisins (seeded and chopped), three pounds of currants (carefully cleaned), one pound of citron (shredded very fine), and one-quarter of a pound of orange peel (chopped very fine). Soak all this prepared fruit in one pint of brandy overnight. Add all to the dough and put in the stiffly-beaten whites last. Bake in a very slow oven for several hours, in cake pans lined with buttered paper. When cold wrap in cloths dipped in brandy and put in earthen jars. If baked in gas oven have light very low. Keep oven the same temperature for four or five hours.

APPLE SAUCE CAKE

This apple sauce cake will be found as delicious and tasty as the rich fruit cake, which is so difficult to prepare, and it is very much less expensive.

In a big mixing bowl, beat to a creamy consistency four tablespoons of butter, one egg and one cup of sugar. Add a saltspoon of salt, one teaspoon of allspice, one teaspoon of vanilla and a little grated nutmeg. Beat and stir all these ingredients well together with the other mixture, then add one cup of chopped raisins, after dusting them with flour. Mix these well through the dough and then add one cup of unsweetened apple sauce which has been pressed through a fine wire sieve. After this is well mixed with the other ingredients, stir in one teaspoon of baking-soda dissolved in one tablespoon of boiling water. Last of all, stir in one cup of flour, sifting twice after measuring it. Bake forty-five minutes in moderate oven.

The tendency in making this cake is to get the dough too thin, therefore the apple sauce should be cooked quite thick, and then if the dough is still too thin add more flour. Bake one hour in moderate oven. This cake can be made with chicken schmalz in place of butter. Ice with plain white frosting.

SPICE CAKE

This spice cake is economical, easy to make and delicious, three qualities which must appeal to the housewife.

Cream one cup of brown sugar and one-half cup of butter (or a little less of any butter substitute). Add one-half teaspoon of ground cloves and ground cinnamon, one cup of sour milk; one teaspoon of baking-soda, two cups of flour and one cup of raisins chopped. Have ready a warm oven and bake three-quarters of an hour.

GREEN TREE LAYER CAKE AND ICING

One cup of granulated sugar, one-half cup of butter, three eggs, one cup of milk, two and one-half scant cups of sifted flour, one teaspoon of vanilla extract, two teaspoons of baking-powder. Cream the butter and sugar together as usual, and then break in three eggs and beat until very creamy. Add the flour and milk alternately, reserving a little of the flour to add after the vanilla and baking-powder. Beat well and bake in layer cake tins. The entire success and lightness of this cake depends upon the beating of the sugar, butter and eggs. If these are beaten long enough they will become as creamy and fluffy as whipped cream.

Icing for This Cake.—One and one-half cups of confectioner's sugar (not powdered), butter the size of a large egg, two tablespoons of cocoa, one teaspoon of vanilla, moisten to make the mixture the consistency of very thick cream. Cream or whipped cream may be used for the mixing, but many like this icing when made with lukewarm coffee. The sugar and butter are creamed together thoroughly and then the cocoa and vanilla are added, and lastly the cream or coffee. This is a good imitation of German tree cake. The icing on tree cake is an inch thick, and it is marked to represent the bark of a tree. The way it is served is with a little green candy on it, and it is really very delicious although extremely rich. The thicker or rather firmer this icing is, the better.

EGGLESS, BUTTERLESS, MILKLESS CAKE

One package of seeded raisins, two cups of sugar, two cups of boiling water, one teaspoon of cinnamon, one teaspoon of cloves, two tablespoons of Crisco, chicken schmalz or clarified drippings, one-half teaspoon of salt. Boil all together five minutes, cool, add one teaspoon of soda dissolved in water, three cups of flour. Bake forty-five minutes, make two cakes in layer pans.

APPLE JELLY CAKE

Rub one cup of butter and two cups of sugar to a cream, add four eggs, whites beaten separately, one cup of milk, two teaspoons of baking-powder and three and one-half cups of flour. Bake in layer tins.

   Filling.—Pare and grate three large apples ("Greenings" preferred), the juice and peel of a lemon, one cup of sugar and one well-beaten egg. Put in ingredients together and boil, stirring constantly until thick. Cool and fill in cake.

CREAM LAYER CAKE

Rub one cup of butter and two scant cups of sugar to a cream; the yolks of four eggs beaten in well, add gradually one cup of milk and three cups of sifted flour, and add three teaspoons of baking-powder in last sifting; put whites in last. Bake in layers as for jelly cake. When cold, spread with the following filling: Moisten two tablespoons of cornstarch with enough cold milk to work it into a paste. Scald one-half pint of milk with one-half cup of sugar and a pinch of salt. Beat the yolks of two eggs light; add the cornstarch to this, and as soon as the milk is scalded pour in the mixture gradually, stirring constantly until thick. Drop in one teaspoon of sweet butter, and when this is mixed in, set away until cool. Spread between layers.

COCOANUT LAYER CAKE

Rub to a cream one-half cup of butter and one and one-half cups of pulverized sugar. Add gradually three eggs, one-half cup of milk and two cups of flour, adding two teaspoons of baking-powder in last sifting. Bake in layers.

Filling.—One grated cocoanut and all of its milk, to half of which add the beaten whites of two eggs and one cup of powdered sugar. Lay this between the layers. Mix with the other half of the grated cocoanut five tablespoons of powdered sugar and strew thickly on top of cake, which has been previously iced.

CHOCOLATE LAYER CAKE

Stir one scant half cup of butter to a cream with one cup of sugar. Add alternately one-half cup of sweet milk, yolks of two eggs which you have previously beaten until quite light, add whites of two, and one-half cup of sifted flour. Make a custard of one-half cup of milk, with one cup of grated chocolate, one-half cup of granulated sugar; boil until thick, add the yolk of one egg, then remove from the fire; stir until cool, add this to the cake batter, add one and one-half cups of sifted flour, two teaspoons of baking-powder and one of vanilla flavoring. Bake in layers and ice between and on top with plain white icing flavored to taste. You may substitute almond or colored icing.

CARAMEL LAYER CAKE

Place one-half cup of sugar in pan over fire. Stir until liquid smokes and burns brown. Add one-half cup of boiling water and cook into syrup. Take one cup butter, one and one-half cups of sugar, yolks of two eggs, over one cup of water and two cups of flour. Beat all thoroughly. Add enough of the burnt sugar to flavor, also one teaspoon of vanilla, another half cup of flour, two teaspoons of baking-powder and whites of two eggs. Bake in two layers, using remainder of burnt sugar for icing.

HUCKLEBERRY CAKE

Stir to a cream one cup of butter and two cups of powdered sugar and add gradually the yolks of four eggs. Sift into this three cups of flour, adding two teaspoons of baking-powder in the last sifting and add one cup of sweet milk alternately with the flour to the creamed butter, sugar and yolks. Spice with one teaspoon of cinnamon and add the stiff-beaten whites of the eggs. Lastly, stir in two cups of huckleberries which have been carefully picked over and well dredged with flour. Be careful in stirring in the huckleberries that you do not bruise them. You will find a wooden spoon the best for this purpose, the edges not being so sharp. Bake in a moderately hot oven; try with a straw, if it comes out clean, your cake is baked. This will keep fresh for a long while.

CREAM PUFFS

One cup of hot water, one-half cup of butter; boil together, and while boiling stir in one cup of sifted flour dry; take from the stove and stir to a thin paste, and after this cools add three eggs unbeaten, and stir vigorously for five minutes. Drop in tablespoonfuls on a buttered tin and bake in a quick oven twenty-five minutes, opening the oven door no oftener than is absolutely necessary, and being careful that they do not touch each other in the pan. This amount will make twelve puffs. Cream for puffs: one cup of milk, one cup of sugar, one egg, three tablespoons of flour, vanilla to flavor. Stir the flour in a little of the milk; boil the rest, turn this in and stir until the whole thickens. When both this and the puffs are cool open the puff a little way with a sharp knife and fill them with the cream.

CHOCOLATE ECLAIRS

To make éclairs spread the batter, prepared as in foregoing recipe, in long ovals and when done cover with plain or chocolate frosting, as follows: Boil one cup of brown sugar with one-half cup of molasses, one tablespoon of butter and two tablespoons of flour. Boil for one-half hour, then stir in one-fourth pound of grated chocolate wet in one-fourth cup of sweet milk and boil until it hardens on the spoon. Flavor with vanilla. Spread this upon the éclairs.

DOBOS TORTE

Cream yolks of six eggs with one-half pound of powdered sugar; add three-fourths cup of flour sifted three times; then add beaten whites of six eggs lightly and carefully into the mixture. Butter pie plates on under side and sprinkle with flour lightly over the butter and spread the mixture very thin. This amount makes one cake of twelve layers. Remove layers at once with a spatula.

Filling.—Cream one-half pound of sweet butter and put on ice immediately; take one-half pound of sweet chocolate and break it into a cup of strong liquid coffee; add one-half pound of granulated sugar and let it boil until you can pull it almost like candy; remove from fire and stir the chocolate until it is quite cold. When cold add the chocolate mixture to the creamed butter. This filling is spread thin between the layers, spread the icing thicker on top and sides of the cake. This is very fine, but care must be taken in baking and removing the layers, as layers are as thin as wafers. Bake and make filling a day or two before needed.

SPONGE CAKE

Weigh any number of eggs, take the same weight of sugar and one-half the weight of flour; the grated rind and juice of one lemon to five eggs. For mixing this cake, see the directions given in "To Bake Cakes"; the mixture should be very light and spongy, great care being used not to break down the whipped whites. The oven should be moderate at first, and the heat increased after a time. The cake must not be moved or jarred while baking. The time will be forty to fifty minutes according to size of cake. Use powdered sugar for sponge-cake. Rose-water makes a good flavoring when a change from lemon is wanted.

SMALL SPONGE CAKES

Separate the whites and yolks of four eggs, beat the whites stiff, and beat into them one-half cup of granulated sugar. Beat the yolks to a very stiff froth and beat into them one-half cup of granulated sugar. This last mixture must be beaten for exactly five minutes. Add the juice and grated rind of one small lemon; beat yolks and whites together well, then stir in very gently one scant cup of flour that has been sifted three times. Remember that every stroke of the spoon after the flour is added toughens the cake just that much, so fold the flour in just enough to mix well. If baked in small patty pans they taste just like lady fingers. Bake twenty or twenty-five minutes in moderate oven.

DOMINOES

Make a sponge cake batter, and bake in long tins, not too large. The batter should not exceed the depth of one-fourth of an inch, spread it evenly and bake it in a quick oven (line the tins with buttered paper). As each cake is taken from the oven, turn it upside down on a clean board or paper. Spread with a thin layer of currant or cranberry jelly, and lay the other cake on top of it. With a hot, sharp knife cut into strips like dominoes; push them with the knife about an inch apart, and ice them with ordinary white icing, putting a tablespoonful on each piece, the heat of the cake will soften it, and with little assistance the edges and sides may be smoothly covered. Set the cakes in a warm place, where the frosting will dry. Make a horn of stiff white paper with just a small opening; at the lower end. Put in one spoon of dark chocolate icing and close the horn at the top, and by pressing out the icing from the small opening, draw a line of it across the centre of each cake, and then make dots like those on dominoes. Keep the horn supplied with the icing.

LADY FINGERS

Beat the yolks of three eggs until light and creamy, add one-quarter pound of powdered sugar (sifted) and continue beating; add flavoring to taste, vanilla, lemon juice, grated rind of lemon or orange. To the whites of the three eggs add one-half saltspoon of salt and beat until very stiff. Stir in lightly one-half cup of flour and then fold in the beaten whites very gently.

Press the mixture through a pastry tube on a baking-tin, covered with paper in portions one-half inch wide by four inches long, or drop on oblong molds; sift a little powdered sugar on top of each cake, and bake from ten to fifteen minutes in a moderate oven. Do not let brown. Remove immediately from pan, brush the flat surface of one cake with white of egg and press the underside of a second cake upon the first.

JELLY ROLL

Take three eggs creamed with one cup of granulated sugar, one cup of flour sifted with two teaspoons of baking-powder, add one-half cup of boiling water. Bake in broad pan—while hot, remove from pan and lay on cloth wet with cold water. Spread with jelly and roll quickly. Sprinkle with powdered sugar.

ANGEL FOOD

Sift one cup of pastry flour once, then measure and sift three times. Add a pinch of salt to the whites of eight or nine eggs or just one cup of whites, beat about one-half, add one-half teaspoon of cream of tartar, then beat the whites until they will stand of their own weight; add one and one-fourth cups of sugar, then flour, not by stirring but folding over and over until thoroughly mixed in; flavor with one-half teaspoon of vanilla or almond extract. Bake in an ungreased pan, patent tube pan preferred. Place the cake in an oven that will just warm it enough through until the batter has raised to the top of the mold, then increase the heat gradually until the cake is well browned over; if by pressing the top of the cake with the finger it will spring back without leaving the imprint of the finger the cake is done through. Great care should be taken that the oven is not too hot to begin with as the cake will rise too fast and settle or fall in the baking. Bake thirty-five to forty minutes. When done, invert the pan; when cool remove from pan.

SUNSHINE CAKE

Beat yolks of five eggs lightly, add one teaspoon of vanilla, or grated rind of one lemon. In another bowl beat seven whites to a froth with a scant one-half teaspoon of cream of tartar, then beat until whites are very stiff. Gradually add one cup of granulated sugar, sifted three times, to the beaten whites. Fold whites and sugar, when beaten, into the beaten yolks. Sift one cup of flour three times, then put into sifter and shake lightly, fold into the cake. Bake forty minutes in ungreased cake pan. As directed for sponge cake invert pan. Remove cake when it has cooled.

MOCHA TORTS

Beat one cup of powdered sugar with the yolks of four eggs; when very light, add one cup of sifted flour in which has been mixed one teaspoon of baking-powder, add three tablespoons of cold water, one-half teaspoon of vanilla, one tablespoon essence of mocha, add the stiffly-beaten whites and bake fifteen to twenty minutes in two layer pans in a moderate oven. Spread when cold with one-half pint of cream to which has been added one tablespoon of mocha essence, one and one-half tablespoon of powdered sugar and then well whipped. Garnish with pounded almonds.

PEACH SHORTCAKE

Make a sponge cake batter of four eggs, one cup of pulverized sugar, a pinch of salt and one cup of flour. Beat the eggs with the sugar until very light. Beat until the consistency of dough and add the grated peel of a lemon, and last the sifted flour. No baking-powder necessary. Bake in jelly tins. Cut the peaches quite fine and sugar bountifully. Put between layers. Eat with cream.

The same recipe may be used for Strawberry Shortcake.

BREMEN APPLE TORTE

Take seven peeled and cored apples, six tablespoons of sugar, two tablespoons of butter, and cook together until apples are soft. Cream six eggs; add to them one pint of sour cream, one tablespoon of vanilla, one-half teaspoon of cinnamon, and sugar to taste; then pour into the cooked apples and let all boil together till thick. Remove from stove. Take three cups of finely rolled zwieback, and in the bottom of a well-greased pan put a layer of two cups of crumbs, then a layer of the apple mixture, a layer of the remaining crumbs, and lastly lumps of butter over all. Bake one hour.

VIENNA PRATER CAKE

Cream the yolks of six eggs with one cup of granulated sugar. Add three-fourths cup of sifted chocolate, three-fourths cup of flour (sifted twice), one and one-half teaspoon of vanilla. Add the beaten whites. Bake thirty minutes. When cold; cut in half and fill with the following: One cup of milk, yolks of two eggs, one cup of chopped walnuts. Boil, stirring constantly to prevent curdling. Sweeten to taste, and after removing from the fire add one tablespoon of rum. Spread while hot.

SAND TORTE

Cream one-half pound of butter with one-half pound of sugar; drop in, one at a time, the yolks of six eggs. Add one small wine glass of rum, one-fourth pound of corn-starch, and one-fourth pound of flour that have been thoroughly mixed; one teaspoon of baking-powder, the beaten whites of six eggs. Bake one hour in a moderate oven.

ALMOND CAKE OR MANDEL TORTE, No. 1

Take one-half pound of almonds and blanch by pouring boiling water over them, and pound in a mortar or grate on grater (the latter is best). Beat yolks of eight eggs vigorously with one cup of sugar, add one-half lemon, grated peel and juice, one tablespoon of brandy, and four lady-fingers grated, the almonds, and fold in the stiffly-beaten whites of eggs. Bake in moderate oven one hour.

ALMOND CAKE OR MANDEL TORTE, No. 2

Take one-fourth pound of sweet almonds and one-eighth pound of bitter ones mixed. Blanch them the day previous to using and then grate or pound them as fine as powder. Beat until light the yolks of nine eggs with eight tablespoons of granulated sugar. Add the grated peel of one lemon and one-half teaspoon of mace or vanilla. Beat long and steadily. Add the grated almonds and continue the stirring in one direction. Add the juice of the lemon to the stiff-beaten whites. Grate four stale lady fingers, add and bake slowly for one hour at least.

BROD TORTE

Take six eggs, seven tablespoons of granulated sugar, seven tablespoons of bread crumbs, one-eighth pound of chopped almonds, one-half teaspoon of allspice, one tablespoon of jelly, grated rind and juice of one lemon, one teaspoon of cinnamon, one-half teaspoon of cloves, one-half wine glass of brandy. Beat yolks of eggs well and add sugar and beat until it blisters, add bread crumbs, almonds, jelly, spice, lemon, and brandy. Then add beaten whites, and bake slowly about forty minutes.

RYE BREAD TORTE

Beat the yolks of four eggs very light with one cup of sugar; add one cup of sifted dry rye bread crumbs to which one teaspoon of baking-powder and a pinch of salt have been added. Moisten one-half cup of ground almonds with two tablespoons of sherry, add and lastly fold in the beaten whites of eggs. Bake in ungreased form in moderate oven.

ZWIEBACK TORTE

Beat the yolks of six eggs with one and one-eighth cups of sugar, add one-half box of zwieback, which has been rolled very fine, add one teaspoon of baking-powder, season with one tablespoon of rum or sherry wine and one-half teaspoon of bitter almond extract. Lastly fold in the stiffly-beaten whites of the six eggs and bake in ungreased form in moderate oven three-quarters of an hour.

CHOCOLATE BROD TORTE

Separate the yolks and whites of ten eggs. Beat the yolks with two cups of pulverized sugar. When thick add one and three-fourth cups of sifted dry rye bread crumbs, one-half pound of sweet almonds, also some bitter ones, grated or powdered as fine as possible, one-fourth pound of citron shredded fine, one cake of chocolate grated, the grated peel of one lemon, the juice of one orange and one lemon, one tablespoon of cinnamon, one teaspoon of allspice, one-half teaspoon of cloves, and a wine glass of brandy. Bake very slowly in ungreased form. Frost with a chocolate icing, made as follows: Melt a small piece of chocolate. Beat the white of an egg stiff with scant cup of sugar, and stir into the melted chocolate and spread with a knife.

BURNT ALMOND TORTE

Beat up four eggs with one cup of sifted powdered sugar. Beat until it looks like a heavy batter. When you think you cannot possibly beat any longer stir one cup of sifted flour with one-half teaspoon of baking-powder. Stir it into batter gradually and lightly, adding three tablespoons of water. Bake in jelly tins. Filling: Scald one-fourth pound of almonds (by pouring boiling water over them), remove skins, put them on a pie plate and set them in the oven to brown slightly. Meanwhile, melt three tablespoons of white sugar, without adding water, stirring it all the while. Stir up the almonds in this, then remove them from the fire and lay on a platter separately to cool. Make an icing of the whites of three eggs beaten very stiff, with one pound of pulverized sugar, and flavor with rose-water. Spread this upon layers and cover each layer with almonds. When finished frost the whole cake, decorating with almonds.

CHOCOLATE TORTE

Take nine eggs, one-half pound of pulverized sugar, one-half pound of almonds, half cut and grated; one-half pound of finest vanilla chocolate grated, one-half pound of raisins, cut and seeded; seven soda crackers, rolled to a powder; one teaspoon of baking-powder, juice of three lemons and one-fourth glass of wine. Beat whites of eggs to a stiff froth and stir in last. Beat yolks with sugar until very light; then add chocolate, and proceed as with other torten.

DATE TORTE

Beat one-half pound of pulverized sugar with the yolks of six large eggs. Beat long and steadily until a thick batter. Add one-half pound of dates, cut very fine, one teaspoon each of allspice and ground cinnamon, one-fourth pound of chocolate grated, juice and peel of one lemon, three and one-half soda crackers, rolled to a fine powder, one teaspoon of baking-powder, and last the stiff-beaten whites. Bake slowly. Cake can be cut in half and put together with jelly.

GERMAN HAZELNUT TORTE

Beat together for twenty minutes until very light the yolks of eight eggs with one-half pound of granulated sugar, then add the very stiffly-beaten whites of eggs, place the bowl in which it has been stirred over a boiler in which water is boiling on the stove, stir continually but slowly until all the batter is well warmed but not too hot, add a small pinch of salt, and one-half pound of grated hazelnuts, add the nuts gradually, mix well and pour into a greased spring form. Bake very slowly. The grated rind of one-half lemon can be added if desired. Ice with boiled icing.

LINZER TORTE

Cream one pound of butter with one pound of sugar until foamy, then add one by one four whole eggs. Mix well, then stir in three-fourths pound of pounded almonds or walnuts, one teaspoon of cinnamon, one-fourth teaspoon of cloves, one pound of flour, one teaspoon of baking-powder, and a few drops of bitter almond essence. Put in four layer pans and bake in slow oven. Put together with apricot, strawberry, or raspberry jam and pineapple marmalade, each layer having a different preserve. Ice top and sides. If only two layers are desired for home use, half the quantity of ingredients can be used. This is a very fine cake. It is better the second day.

RUSSIAN PUNCH TORTE

Bake three layers of almond tart and flavor it with a wine glass of arrack. When baked, scrape part of the cake out of the thickest layer, not disturbing the rim, and reserve these crumbs to add to the following filling: Boil one-half pound of sugar in one-fourth cup of water until it spins a thread. Add to this syrup a wine glass of rum, and the crumbs, and spread over the layers, piling one on top of the other. Another way to fill this cake is to take some crab-apple jelly or apple marmalade and thin it with a little brandy.

WALNUT TORTE, No. 1

Grate eight ounces of walnuts and eight ounces of blanched almonds. Beat light the yolks of twelve eggs and three-fourths pound of sugar. Add the grated nuts and one-fourth pound of sifted flour, fold in the whites beaten to a stiff froth. Bake in layers and fill with sweetened whipped cream.

WALNUT TORTE, No. 2

Separate the yolks and whites of six eggs, being very careful not to get a particle of the yolks into the whites. Sift one-half pound of granulated sugar into the yolks and beat until thick as batter. Add a pinch of salt to the whites and beat very stiff. Have ready one-fourth pound of grated walnuts, reserve whole pieces for decorating the top of cake. Add the pounded nuts to the beaten yolks, and two tablespoons of grated lady fingers or stale sponge cake. Last add the stiffly-beaten whites of the eggs. Bake in layers and fill with almond or plain icing.

CHESTNUT TORTE

Boil one pound of chestnuts in the shells, peel them while warm, put nuts through potato ricer or colander. Beat well the yolks of six eggs with six tablespoons of sugar, add all the chestnut purée but two or three tablespoons reserved for top of torte, then add three teaspoons of baking-powder and the well-beaten whites of the six eggs; bake in moderate oven fifteen to twenty minutes. Whip one-half pint of cream, add to this the chestnut purée which was reserved, and a little sugar; garnish torte with this mixture. Enough for twelve persons.

NUT HONEY CAKE

Mix two cups of brown sugar, two cups of honey, six egg yolks and beat them thoroughly. Sift together three cups of flour, one-quarter teaspoon of salt, three teaspoons of ground cinnamon, one-half teaspoon each of ground cloves, ground nutmeg and allspice, and one and one-half teaspoons of soda; add one cup of chopped raisins, one-half ounce of citron cut in small pieces, one-half ounce of candied orange peel cut in small pieces, one-half pound of almonds coarsely chopped. Beat the whites of three eggs very stiff and add them last. Pour the dough to the depth of about half an inch into well-buttered tins and bake in a slow oven for one-half hour.

ICINGS AND FILLINGS FOR CAKES

BOILED ICING

One cup of sugar, one-third cup of boiling water, white of one egg beaten stiff. Pour water on sugar until dissolved, heat slowly to boiling point without stirring; boil until syrup will thread when dropped from tip of spoon; as soon as it threads, pour slowly over beaten white, then beat with heavy wire spoon until of proper consistency to spread. Flavor.

WHITE CARAMEL ICING

Put on to boil two cups of brown sugar, one cup of milk and a small lump of butter. Boil until it gets as thick as cream, then beat with a fork or egg whip until thick and creamy. Spread quickly on cake.

MAPLE SUGAR ICING

Boil two cups of maple sugar with one-half cup of boiling water until it threads from the spoon. Pour it upon the beaten whites of two eggs and beat until cold. Spread between layers and on top of cake. Do not make icings on cloudy or rainy days.

UNBOILED ICING

Take the white of one egg and add to it the same quantity of water (measure in an egg shell). Stir into this as much confectioner's sugar to make it of the right consistency to spread upon the cake. Flavor with any flavoring desired. You may color it as you would boiled frosting by adding fruit coloring.

COCOANUT ICING

Mix cocoanut with the unboiled icing. If you desire to spread it between the cakes, scatter more cocoanut over and between the layers.

NUT ICING

Mix any quantity of finely chopped nuts into any quantity of cream icing (unboiled) as in the foregoing recipes. Ice the top of cake with plain icing, and lay the halves of walnuts on top.

ORANGE ICING

Grate the peel of one-half orange, mix with two tablespoons of orange juice and one tablespoon of lemon juice and let stand fifteen minutes. Strain and add to the beaten yolk of one egg. Stir in enough powdered sugar to make it the right consistency to spread upon the cake.

CHOCOLATE GLAZING

Grate two sticks of bitter chocolate, add five tablespoons of powdered sugar and three tablespoons of boiling water. Put on the stove, over moderate fire, stir while boiling until smooth, glossy and thick. Spread at once on cake and set aside to harden.

CHOCOLATE ICING, UNBOILED

Beat the whites of three eggs and one and one-half cups of pulverized sugar, added gradually while beating. Beat until very thick, then add four tablespoons of grated chocolate and two teaspoons of vanilla.

This quantity is sufficient for a very large cake.

INSTANTANEOUS FROSTING

To the white of an unbeaten egg add one and one-fourth cups of pulverized sugar and stir until smooth. Add three drops of rose-water, ten of vanilla, and the juice of half a lemon. It will at once become very white, and will harden in five or six minutes.

PLAIN FROSTING

To one cup of confectioner's sugar add some liquid, either milk or water, to make it the right consistency to spread, flavor with vanilla. Instead of the water or milk, orange juice can be used. A little of the rind must be added. Lemon juice can be substituted in place of vanilla. Chocolate melted over hot water and added to the sugar and water makes a nice chocolate icing; flavor with vanilla.

ALMOND ICING

Take the whites of two eggs and one-half pound of sweet almonds, which should be blanched, dried and grated or pounded to a paste. Beat the whites of the eggs, add half a pound of confectioner's sugar, one tablespoon at a time, until all is used, and then add the almonds and a few drops of rosewater. Spread between or on top of cake. Put on thick, and when nearly dry cover with a plain icing. If the cakes are well dredged with a little flour after baking, and then carefully wiped before the icing is put on, it will not run and can be spread more smoothly. Put the frosting in the centre of the cake, dip a knife in cold water and spread from the centre toward the edge.

MOCHA FROSTING

One cup of pulverized sugar into which sift two dessertspoons of dry cocoa, two tablespoons of strong hot coffee in which is melted a piece of butter the size of a walnut. Beat well and add a little vanilla.

MARSHMALLOW FILLING

Melt one-half pound marshmallows over hot water, cook together one cup of sugar and one-quarter cup of cold water until it threads thoroughly. Beat up the white of an egg and syrup and mix, then add to the melted marshmallows and beat until creamy and cool. Can be used for cake filling or spread between two cookies.

FIG FILLING

One pound of figs chopped fine, one cup of water, one-half cup of sugar; cook all together until soft and smooth.

BANANA FILLING

Mash six bananas, add juice of one lemon and three or more tablespoons of sugar; or add mashed bananas with whipped cream or boiled icing.

CREAM FILLING

Scald two cups of milk. Mix together three-fourths of a cup of sugar, one-third cup of flour and one-eighth teaspoon of salt. Add to three slightly-beaten eggs and pour in scalded milk. Cook twenty minutes over boiling water, stirring constantly until thickened. Cool and flavor. This can be used as a foundation for most fillings, by adding melted chocolate, nuts, fruits, etc.

COFFEE FILLING

Put three cups of warmed-over or freshly made coffee in a small casserole, add two tablespoons of powdered sugar, one-half teaspoon of vanilla. When at boiling point (do not let it boil), add one cup of milk or cream. Then add one tablespoon of cornstarch which has been moistened with cold water. Stir in while cooking till it is smooth and glossy. When the cake is cool, pour mixture over the layers.

LEMON JELLY FOR LAYER CAKE

Take one pound of sugar, yolks of eight eggs with two whole ones, the juice of five large lemons, the grated peel of two, and one-quarter pound of butter. Put the sugar, lemon and butter into saucepan and melt over a gentle fire. When all is dissolved, stir in the eggs which have been beaten, stir rapidly until it is thick as honey, and spread some of this between the layers of cake. Pack the remainder in jelly glasses.

LEMON PEEL

Keep a wide-mouthed bottle of brandy in which to throw lemon peel. Often you will have use for the juice of lemons only. Then it will be economical to put the lemon peel in the bottle to use for flavoring. A teaspoon of this is sufficient for the largest cake.

LEMON EXTRACT

Take the peel of half a dozen lemons and put in alcohol the same as for vanilla.

VANILLA EXTRACT

Take two ounces of vanilla bean and one of tonka. Soak the tonka in warm water until the skin can be rubbed off; then cut or chop in small pieces and put in two wine bottles. Fill with half alcohol, half water; cork, seal, and in a week's time will be ready for use.